LOL

summersdale

LOL

Summersdale Publishers Ltd
46 West Street
Chichester
West Sussex
PO19 1RP
UK

www.summersdale.com

Printed and bound in China

ISBN: 978-1-84953-486-4

Substantial discounts on bulk quantities of Summersdale books are available to corporations, professional associations and other organisations. For details contact Nicky Douglas by telephone: +44 (0) 1243 756902, fax: +44 (0) 1243 786300 or email: nicky@summersdale.com.

INTRODUCTION

Thanks to the Internet, we can now share information across the globe in seconds, and not just the unimportant stuff like share prices and train timetables: a constant stream of jokes, rude remarks and pictures of kittens means we can all laugh out loud whenever we switch on. And we can signal our joy to fellow screen-addicts with the universally-recognised acronym of fun: LOL!

From crocodiles to cowboys, and from rubber ducks to unicorns, this playful collection of funny facts will ensure that you get your daily giggle even when you're not online.

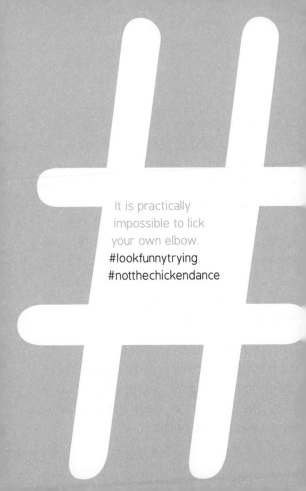

It is practically
impossible to lick
your own elbow.
#lookfunnytrying
#notthechickendance

Crocodiles are unable to
stick their tongues out.
#mustbealltheteeth

#lol

In Blythe, California, you may only wear cowboy boots if you own at least two cows.
#thesebootsaremadeforcowboys

#LOL

The first ever television remote was called 'Lazy Bones' – they knew their stuff!
#somethingsneverchange
#passthelazybones

#LOL

In Montana, a would-be robber entered a restaurant, broke down in tears and was given a pizza by the sympathetic staff. #whosaidcrimedoesntpay

When a new pope is ordained, the cardinals have to look under his robes and check he has testicles.

#definitelynotagirl

5 September is Be Late for Something Day. Don't forget to forget to set your alarm for it!
#betterlatethanontime

The Statue of Liberty's
sandals are size 879.
#areyousayingivegotbigfeet?

A vending machine at the National University of Singapore gave out free cola to people who hugged it.
#sharethelove
#lovemachine

The planet Saturn would float if you had a big enough bathtub to put it in.
#betterthanarubberduck

Jellyfish are technically not fish.
They are also technically not jelly.
#liesliesalllies

The world record for ferret legging (keeping ferrets down your trousers) is 5 hours and 30 minutes.
#ouchOUCHowowowOWWWWW

Stuffing your nostrils with raw bacon can stop serious nosebleeds. **#couldsaveyourbacon**

In France, in 1386, a pig
was executed for murder.
#couldntsavehisbacon

#lol

The name for a male turkey is a gobbler.
#doeswhatitsaysonthetin

The original tablecloths were designed, not to protect the table, but for diners to wipe their hands and faces on. Try doing that on your grandma's best one!
#dontstandupwhilewiping
#crash!

#LOL

The south-western coast of Africa is home to penguins called jackass penguins.
#youshouldhearwhattheycallus

'Traditional' fortune cookies were not invented in China. They were first made in America, in 1918, by Charles Jung.

#goingoutforanamerican

There is an actual protein
called sonic hedgehog
homolog.
#whatnext?
#supermarioprotein?

The word 'avocado' is
derived from 'ahuacatl',
which also means 'testicle'.
#illhaveatesticlesaladplease

In Brazil, there is a breed
of spider whose bite can
cause an erection which
lasts for hours.
#painfullyembarrassing

School buses in Japan
are designed to look like
cartoons, including Pokemon
and cute cats.
#coolschool

A group of unicorns is known as a blessing.
#youdhavetohaveonetoseethose

Brit Colin Furze has the fastest mobility scooter in the world. His modified scooter can reach speeds of over 70 mph! #hypermobile

The Bible has been translated into many languages, including Klingon! #spacemissionaries

David Morgan of Bedford, UK, owns the world's largest collection of traffic cones. He has examples of about two-thirds of all the traffic cones ever made.
#adivertingcollection

#lol

There is a World Record for fastest dog on a skateboard! It is held by Tillman, a bulldog from the USA, who skateboarded 100 m in less than 20 seconds.
#radicaldog

#LOL

Flies are completely deaf.
#nowondertheyalwaysignoreme
#thatexplainsthelackofconversation

The World Record for fastest 100 m on a spacehopper belongs to Ashrita Furman, at just over 30 seconds.
#gethopping!

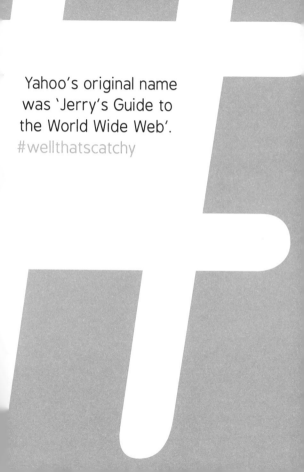

Yahoo's original name was 'Jerry's Guide to the World Wide Web'.
#wellthatscatchy

Charlotte Lee owns the world's largest collection of rubber ducks. She has been collecting since 1996 and has 5,631. #whatabathfull!

The Cookie Monster
has a name: Sid.
#whoareyoucallingamonster
#butidolovecookies

There is a prison
in Uruguay called
'Freedom'.
#addinginsulttoinjury

Michael Keaton is actually called Michael Douglas.
#famousnametwins
#howdoesthathappen?

Rats will laugh when tickled.
#squeee!
#guesstheyhaveasenseofhumour

In certain parts of France, it is illegal to die.
#cantreallycometoyourowndefence
#notliketheycanexecuteyouforit!

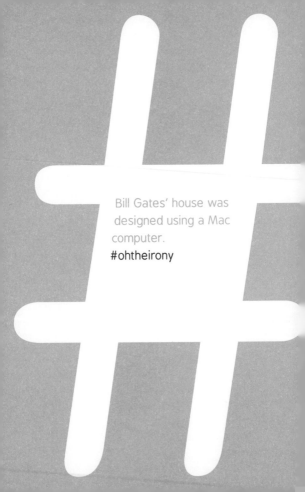

Bill Gates' house was
designed using a Mac
computer.
#ohtheirony

Hitler was nominated for the
Nobel Peace Prize in 1939.
#thinkwemadeamistakethere

#lol

In Japan, there are vending machines selling wigs for dogs.
#whoareyoutryingtofool?
#thatsadachshundnotanafghan!

#LOL

The group noun for
ferrets is a 'business'.
#ferretsinsuitsneedisaymore?

Not as fruitless as it might seem, banging your head against a brick wall burns 150 calories per hour.
#nopainnogain
#anyonegotanyparacetamol?

Swearing can help relieve pain, as long as it isn't overused.
#pardonmylanguage
#doctorsorders

A cat is unable to see
under its own nose.
#youvegotalittlemilkthere
#where?
#nevermind

In the 1970s, a Barbie doll was released that grew boobs. Once wasn't enough — another was released in the 2000s. #growingpains

In 2011, a cat named Sal from Boston was summoned for jury service. When his owners pointed out he was a cat, the court ruled he still had to appear!
#guiltyornotguilty?
#miaow

In Quitman, Georgia, it is illegal for a chicken to cross the road.

#whydidthe…oh

The lollipop was named after its inventor's favourite racehorse, Lolly Pop.
#luckyitwasntcalleddobbin

Stuffed toys such as teddy bears
kill more people than actual bears.
#donotcuddlethebears

In 2004, Barbie
and Ken broke up.
#itsnotmeitsyou...

In one area of India, in 2004, policemen were given pay increases if they grew moustaches.

#mous-cash

#lol

In France, it is illegal to name a pig 'Napoleon'.
#pigtator
#NapoleonBonepork

#LOL

Herring really do talk out of their backsides: they communicate using farts!
#pardonme
#iwasjustsayinghi

On average, a budgie will poo every 15 minutes.
#niceandregular

The 'blood' in Hitchcock's *Psycho* was actually chocolate syrup.
#sweetdemise

In India, it is legal for a man
marry a dog.
#doyoutakethisdog
#forricherforpawer

The human brain operates on about the same amount of energy as a 10 watt bulb.

#notthebrightestbulb

Apparently, the most uneventful, boring day of the twentieth century was 11 April 1954. #interestingdaydear? #notreally

If you plan a route on Google Maps between Japan and China, step 44 tells you to 'Jet-ski across the Pacific Ocean'.

#mapswithasenseofhumour

It is illegal to mow your front lawn
dressed as Elvis in Switzerland.
#banggomyplansfortheweekend

The longest domain name in the world is www.thelongestdomain-nameintheworldandthensomeand-thensomemoreandmore.com.
#wouldnthaveguessedthatone

Ringo Starr originally
wanted to be
a hairdresser.
#illhavethebowlcut

It is illegal to catch mice
in Cleveland, Ohio, unless
you have a hunting licence.
#mustneedatinygunforthat

#lol

On Facebook, one of the language options is 'Pirate'.
#yarrmehearties

The American national anthem got its melody from an old British drinking song.
#starspangledbeerglass

The tin can was invented 30 years before the can opener.
#willthiskeepfor30years

A study in 2006
revealed that mice
do NOT like cheese!
#ironystrikesagain

The ghosts in Pac-Man have names: Blinky, Pinky, Inky and Clyde.
#rightturnclyde

The name for a group of rats is a 'mischief'.
#givearatabadname

LOL

In the 1983 film *Jaws 3D*, when the shark explodes, some of its 'guts' are actually ET stuffed toys.
#alieninalienenvironment

It is possible for pigs to suffer from mysophobia, aka fear of dirt!
#OCDpig

Mosquitoes only take around 15 seconds to mate.
#howwasitforyou?
#howwaswhat?

In 1920, the tug-of-war was counted as an Olympic sport! #heaveho!

In Tibet, Buddhist monasteries see pugs as religious symbols. #sopuglyitscute

In the original *Halloween* film, the mask worn by Michael Myers is a Captain Kirk mask, painted white.
#face:thefinalfrontier

#lol

Human tonsils can be bounced higher than a similarly sized rubber ball, but only for the first half hour after removal.
#tonsiltennisanyone?

#LOL

The line 'Knock knock! Who's there?' was first coined by Shakespeare in *Macbeth*.

#shakespearewho?

In 2006, a Sudanese man caught *in flagrante* with a neighbour's goat was forced to marry the animal and pay a dowry of $50 to the owner.

#loveisblind

Napalm Death hold the record for the shortest song ever recorded. *You Suffer* is 1.316 seconds long.

#worthit?
#probablynot

Michel Lotito, aka
Monsieur Mangetout,
ate many inanimate objects,
including a whole aeroplane.
#appetitefordestruction
#heavymetaldietplan

Frank Oz voiced both Yoda and Miss Piggy.
#ajokethismustbe

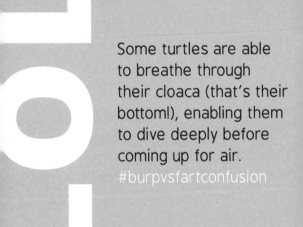

Some turtles are able to breathe through their cloaca (that's their bottom!), enabling them to dive deeply before coming up for air.
#burpvsfartconfusion

The man who invented the Pringles can had his ashes buried inside one.
#thatsdedication
#hepoppedandstopped

Neilasparophobia is fear of aliens.
#soundsmorelikefearofneilsass

Research by the UK Tea Council found that drinking tea was good for your teeth.
#theywouldsaythatwouldntthey

In the film
Singin' in the Rain,
the rain is
actually milk.
#singininthemilk

The honey badger is listed in the *Guinness World Records* as the world's most fearless creature.
#honeybadgerdontcare

#lol

The famed Beatles song *Yesterday* was originally going to be called *Scrambled Eggs*.
#allmybreakfastsseemedsofaraway

#LOL

In France, there is a
soft drink called *Pschitt*.
#suchanelegantlanguage

In the film *The Karate Kid*, Daniel actually learns kung fu, not karate.

#thekungfukid
#getyourfactsstraight

Though he invented the telephone, Alexander Graham Bell never called his wife or his mother, as they were both deaf.
#hello?Hello?HELLO??

The word 'verb' is a noun.
#grammarconfusion

Not only is Uranus gassy,
it's also completely
tilted to one side!
#musthavebeenthecabbage

If you're interested in finding out
more about our books,
find us on Facebook at
Summersdale Publishers
and follow us on Twitter at
@Summersdale.

www.summersdale.com